THE
CROSSING
Rite of Passage
FROM
BOYHOOD TO MANHOOD

YOUNG MEN'S MANUAL

THE
CROSSING
Rite of Passage
FROM
BOYHOOD TO MANHOOD

YOUNG MEN'S MANUAL

RICHARD RUPP

WayPoint Books

The Crossing Rite of Passage
from Boyhood to Manhood:
Young Men's Manual

WayPoint Books

www.thecrossingriteofpassage.com

ISBN-13: 978-0692134214
ISBN-10: 0692134212

To my son Jordan
with all my love and pride.

CONTENTS

ACKNOWLEDGMENTS

Fair Winds to the boys who crossed into manhood on our first initiation sail to Catalina Island. Your journey was the start for this book and mission to raise other great men.
Christopher, Matthew, Eric and Jordan—
may you be the first of a million new men to come.

Introduction

Major League baseball players never start a new season without spring training. Like all athletes, they need coaching, training and practice to succeed. They also need character qualities like confidence, courage, commitment and discipline. As your new season of manhood is about to begin, you also need coaching to succeed. Character qualities like discipline, responsibility and self-control will also be required. Your season of boyhood is coming to a close. Boyhood is not meant to last forever. Your destiny is manhood, and this coaching program will help take you there. The Crossing Rite of Passage is your own spring training for great manhood.

Without guidance and training from older men, many guys never become mature men. We all know men who never grew up. Boys don't become men just by growing older. Like Peter Pan and the Lost Boys, some boys never grow up and get lost in Never Land. Or like the true story of sailor Richard Pham, they end up thousands of miles off course to their destiny.

One spring day in Southern California, Pham set sail by himself from Long Beach to Catalina Island. The crossing is less than twenty-five miles. The sail takes around five hours. But Pham never made it there. He totally disappeared. Four months later and 2,500 miles south of Catalina, a U.S. Navy ship rescued Pham in his battered sailboat—drifting 300 miles off Costa Rica. On his way to Catalina, a sudden storm broke his mast in half. His outboard motor and radio also died. Drifting south with the wind and current, he had no food, no radio contact, and no water. He survived by eating turtles and a sea gull.[1]

The Crossing Rite of Passage from Boyhood to Manhood will keep you on your course to manhood. Your Mentor Team will make sure that you arrive. Too many guys end up like Pham because they weren't prepared enough for the journey. Their lives keep drifting south. Nearly two million men have drifted as far south into the ultimate shipwreck of prison. Millions more have problems with commitment and marriage. Misguided men often get hooked on drugs, alcohol, food or sex to cope with their feelings of pain and loneliness. They sail alone through life and don't talk with anyone for help and support.

Boys need men and mentors to care for them and guide them to a better life. They need men whom they can talk with and trust. Boys need training in character qualities like responsibility, commitment and self-control. This rite of passage will give you all these things. You and a team of boys will have a team of fathers and mentors to prepare you for manhood. Your Mentor Team will be your own coaching staff.

The men will train you to become a young man of faith, courage, and purpose. Their lessons will help you succeed in school and life, and even as a husband and father someday. The lessons will also help keep you out of prison and trouble. Drawing upon the traditions of the Jewish Bar Mitzvah, tribal initiation rituals, Christian Sacraments and biblical teachings, this training equips you for a great Christian manhood.

Your Mentor Team will teach you six practical Lessons in Manhood, starting with how Jesus is the ultimate model for men. Next you will discover your mission in life and create a personal code of honor to guide your daily conduct. You will learn to bless others like a King, to protect others as a Warrior, and to treat girls and women with care and respect. The Good Deed project teaches how great manhood serves others and gives more than it takes.

You will also learn your role in the epic story of the Christian faith.

To strengthen your courage and confidence as a man, the Mentor Team will take your team of boys outdoors on an Adventure Challenge. Your team will climb a mountain, kayak down a river or sail at sea. After your hike, bike, climb or sail, the Challenge culminates with a campout and night-time initiation ceremony around a fire. Finally, your rite of passage concludes in a church ceremony where you will contribute to the church service and be recognized as a new man.

Christian boys have a great advantage in their journey to manhood. They have a perfect example to lead them. Jesus said that he is "the Way, the Truth and the Life." (John 14:6) And just as He called his disciples to "follow me," He says the same to you. This rite of passage will help you to hear Christ's voice and follow him into great manhood. You don't need to drift off course in life. Christ will be your Way and compass every day.

The Young Men's Manual begins with three chapters about rites of passage. Throughout history and throughout the world, boys have had a rite of passage to transform them into men. Through ritual and instruction from older men, boys learn new responsibilities and skills as men. New young men are taught how to protect and provide for their tribe or people. They learn character qualities like courage, commitment and self-control. From tribal initiations in Africa to the Jewish Bar Mitzvah, all rites of passage train boys to become responsible new men.

Read each of the six Lessons in Manhood before your Mentor Team meetings. Write your answers in this book before or during each meeting. Keep this Manual together with your favorite books. Remember to reread your notes and lessons every year until you reach seventeen. These lessons will help keep you on

God's best path for your life and manhood. Study the Scriptures for Christian manhood at the back of the book. Even better, memorize some of them to give you wisdom and keep you on course in life. The Bible will help you make better choices.

After the season when boys will be boys, there comes the season—and choice—to become a man. The apostle Paul said, "When I was a child, I thought like a child, I spoke like a child, I reasoned as a child. When I became a man, I put childish ways behind me." (I Cor.13:11) Manhood is always a choice.

Your destiny as a man awaits you. Your boyhood is ending. A lifetime adventure lies ahead. More faith, courage and responsibilities are calling you. It's time to take the field. You've been called up from the Minors to the Majors now, from boyhood to manhood—drafted, picked and chosen by God and men. Get ready for a new season in life! Your spring training has begun.

The Crossing Rite of Passage
from Boyhood to Manhood

Training Calendar

Check off each box and write the date as the event is completed.

Completed   Event

Mentor Team Lessons in Manhood

☐ _____ 1. Crossing from Boyhood to Manhood
☐ _____ 2. Jesus: The Model for Great Manhood
☐ _____ 3. Manhood with a Mission and Code of Honor
☐ _____ 4. The Manhood of a King: To Bless & Serve
☐ _____ 5. The Manhood of a Warrior: To Protect & Fight
☐ _____ 6. Manhood with Care & Respect for Women

☐ _____ Your Role in God's Epic Story

☐ _____ Good Deed Service Project

☐ _____ Adventure Challenge

☐ _____ Mentor Team Initiation with Fire Ceremony

☐ _____ Church Initiation Ceremony

I

"Today I am a Man": The Jewish Bar Mitzvah

This Saturday morning new men will walk out of synagogues all over the world. Although they just turned thirteen years old, these Jewish boys will boldly proclaim in their Bar Mitzvah services that, "Today, I am a man." Manhood has begun.

But how can an adolescent really call himself a man? And how can his family and community really believe he's a man? At this age he is not old enough to vote, smoke, drive or marry. Yet in Jewish tradition, the age of thirteen changes a boy into a man because he is now old enough to do the *one* thing that makes him a man for the rest of his life. He is now morally responsible to follow God's commandments. Bar Mitzvah literally means Son (Bar) of the Commandment (Mitzvah). Jewish manhood is uniquely defined as living a moral and godly life.

Before thirteen, Jewish children are encouraged to obey God's commandments. But upon turning thirteen, every child becomes obligated to obey the commandments. From then on a boy must face the two opposing forces within every person's

16

nature, the *yester hatov* (good inclination) and the *yester hara* (evil inclination). Life becomes a daily battle to choose good over evil. In Jewish belief, the biggest fight of your life is not outside of yourself. The biggest fight is within.

The apostle Paul wrote about this battle within his own Jewish/Christian life. "So I find this law at work: When I want to do good, evil is right there with me. For in my inner being I delight in God's law, but I see another law at work in the members of my body, waging war against the law of my mind....Therefore, brothers, we have an obligation—but it is not to the sinful nature, to live according to it." (Romans 7:21-23, 8:12) Paul has a thoroughly Jewish sense of obligation to the commandments when he tells the Roman Christians, "Hate what is evil; cling to what is good...Do not be overcome by evil, but overcome evil with good."(Rom. 12:9, 21) As a Jewish boy who grew up in the most Orthodox of Jewish traditions, Paul lived his life as a Son of the Commandment until the day he died—while at the same time clearly teaching that he was saved by grace, not by his works. (Eph.2:8-10)

Parents are no longer morally responsible

The Bar Mitzvah is not only a moral turning point for the thirteen year old boy. The day is also a turning point for his parents. Their previous responsibility for their son's moral life changes. The son is now responsible for his own moral choices in life. To recognize this change, the father says a prayer in his son's Bar Mitzvah ceremony, *"Baruch she-petarani me-onsho shel zeh"* ("Blessed is the One Who has now freed me from responsibility for this one") He thanks God that he is no longer responsible for his son's sins. Rabbi Jeffrey Salkin explains the moment.

"It is also a kind of cosmic sigh—an admission that even sincere, competent, highly committed parents are limited in what they can do with their children. The rest is up to the child himself or herself. When parents say Baruch she-peterani, they say, in effect, "Whatever this young person does now, he is legally and morally culpable. Thank God, it's not my responsibility. At that moment, the parent becomes like Isaac, who, upon looking at their sons, Jacob and Esau, realized that he had done all that he could for them. One son would worship God, the other would worship idols. There are limits to every parent's hopes and dreams, limits to every parent's ability to control and influence. The rest is up to faith, hope, and trust."[2]

With his father's declaration, a son understands that ultimate responsibility for his life and faith lies in his own hands now—not with his parents or anyone else.

A man must leave his father and mother

The Bar Mitzvah also recognizes a boy's growing independence from his parents, which is a key task of adolescence. The ritual supports a boy's sense of his own identity, autonomy and emotional separation from them. The ceremony is a good reminder to parents that their days with their sons are numbered. They must prepare to see him as a man now—even at age thirteen. Jewish parents get choked up at their son's Bar Mitzvah, with many shedding tears of pride, loss and appreciation that their sons have grown up. Support for their son's separation and manhood also helps Jewish boys in future marriage. As written in Genesis, "For this reason a man will leave his father and his mother, and be united with his wife." (Gen.2:24 NIV) Every man must grow up and leave his parents before he can successfully unite with his wife. In Jewish tradition, thirteen is the time to start leaving.

Jesus himself separated from his parents at age twelve. Literally. For three days they didn't know where he was. After their annual trip to Jerusalem for Passover, Jesus decided to stay behind at the Temple to talk with the rabbis. When his parents finally found him, they were probably shocked at his response; "Why were you searching for me? Didn't you know that I had to be in my Father's house?" Jesus didn't stay behind to hang out with friends or get into trouble. Instead, he was already acting like a man "in the temple courts, sitting among the teachers, listening to them and asking them questions. Everyone who heard him was amazed at his understanding and his answers. When his parents saw him, they were astonished."(Lu. 2:46-48)

Most parents would also be astonished if their thirteen year old sons couldn't get enough of their synagogue or church. At the age of twelve, Jesus started an active role in his contribution to Temple life. The Bar Mitzvah requires the same involvement of all Jewish boys.

Young men have a role in their synagogue

Jewish tradition recognizes that thirteen is the age of religious responsibility. The young man has the new right to help lead religious services and to count in a minyan (the quorum of ten men and women needed to perform parts of services). With this new authority, the boy understands he is needed and has a vital role in his synagogue. He goes to services not just for his own sake, but also for the community's sake.

Most thirteen year old Christian boys are not taught that they are needed in their church. In fact, most churches don't ask or expect young teenagers to contribute anything to their church services. Churches can learn from the ancient Jewish tradition. The Bar Mitzvah sends a powerful message to boys that their synagogue needs them. Christian boys need to hear the same from their churches too. Churches needs their contribution.

The Bar Mitzvah also reminds the entire congregation about the heart of their Jewish faith and practice. Rabbi Salkin observes that the Bar Mitzvah developed out of God's covenant with Israel. "The mitzvoth (commandments) are our end of the covenant. Mitzvah, in fact, is one of the most important ideas Judaism gave to the world: a relationship with God entails mutual responsibility."[3] There are 613 commandments in the Torah. The two most common ones require ritual observance of the Sabbath and eating kosher foods. Other mitzvoth include prohibitions like not stealing or murdering, and positive commands like helping the poor and the sick. Rabbi Salkin continues, "The significance of Bar Mitzvah in Jewish life cannot be underestimated. It is central to Jewish identity, which is all about a daily relationship with God and following his commands. It is the essence of the Covenant, our end of the agreement made at Sinai, the summit of Jewish existence."[4]

Jewish boys train with their rabbis for years before their Bar Mitzvah ceremony. They study the Bible and learn Jewish theology, traditions and commandments. They learn Hebrew and practice reading their assigned biblical passages and blessings in Hebrew.

The date for a boy's Bar Mitzvah is easy to remember. The ceremony is held on the first Sabbath after his thirteenth birthday. The ceremony takes place during the regular Saturday morning synagogue service in order that the whole community is present for the event.

Since the sixteenth century to today, several rituals are now customary in the Bar Mitzvah service. The boy's responsibilities in the service include:

Reciting the Blessings from the Torah

Reading or chanting that week's Torah portion in Hebrew

Reading from the Haftarah (the Prophets) in Hebrew

A brief sermon (around five minutes) on the Scripture lesson

Leading the congregation in prayer

Giving thanks to his parents and Rabbi for preparing him for this day

The boy's family, relatives, and friends also play a part in the service. Each of these loved ones takes a turn offering a special blessing before each of the eight readings from the Torah. Father and mother give their personal words of blessing for their son. Presents are given to the boy during the service from family and the congregation. Finally, a reception follows the service where everyone personally congratulates the boy for officially becoming a man.

Jewish tradition, tribal societies, and the example of Jesus all recognize thirteen year olds as young men. In these traditions, adolescence is not just a time to party and have fun. It's not a stage of defiance toward adults, authorities or laws. Rather, adolescence is the beginning of a responsible and godly adulthood. It is a time to learn values, character qualities and skills that make a contribution to the world. Jesus started his own adult life at age twelve. Christian boys can too.

2

Tribal Rites of Passage into Manhood

Painful and bloody. In tribal cultures around the world, the rite of passage from boyhood to manhood feels like torture. Tribal initiations train boys to become warriors. They are painful to teach them courage and to endure pain in war. To be a man is to be a warrior. Since time began and in every culture, a man's universal role and responsibility is to protect his tribe, land, women and children. Warrior manhood isn't selfish. It mean's laying down one's life for others.

After they are beaten in their initiation, the boys in Sambia, New Guinea have sharp grasses jammed up their noses until they are covered in blood. Boys from the American Indian Tewa tribe in New Mexico carry permanent scars from their ritual beatings with yucca whips. Twelve year old boys in East Africa endure the worst pain of all. As they are circumcised by the men with knives, the boys are forbidden to flinch or make a sound. Many of these boys tragically bleed to death. Those who cry out or even blink an eye are shamed as unworthy of manhood by their tribe.[5] Such restrictions of intense emotions and pain will sadly cause boys to shut off from their emotions as men. Other boys around the world have a tooth knocked out or a finger cut off. Their scars are lifetime reminders that they are now men—warrior men. Boyhood is over.

No More Mamas' Boys

The comfortable life with mother is also over. Another major purpose of tribal rites of passage is to separate a boy from being overly close to his mother and to connect him with men. Boys cannot become men unless they leave their boyhood dependency on mother behind. Boys learn to bond and identify with men and their masculinity.

While women can raise babies into boyhood, boys need men to transform them into manhood. If boyhood was a time for milk and cookies and fun, manhood is a time for work and sacrifice (but also time for fun!). If boyhood is about taking, manhood is about giving and serving. The time must come in every boy's life to choose between boyhood and manhood. In contrast to their African and Indian brothers, many American boys are never forced to choose between the two. They often stay mama's boys.

An American Peace Corps teacher in Africa was once asked how the men of his tribe in America "called him out" from his mother's house and into manhood. Since the teacher had no idea what his African student meant, he asked him to explain. The student said that after a boyhood of growing up in his mother's hut, a boy's twelfth birthday brings a life-changing choice. The men of the tribe come to get him. Arriving with their torches in the night, with loud cries and drums they pound and pound on his mother's door to "Come out!" The time has come for the boy to leave his mother and boyhood behind. In that one moment, he must choose to leave her and become a man among his tribe. When he opens the door, while his mother is crying and wailing, the men seize the boy and take him away from her and her village for weeks.[6] Some tribes keep the boys away for three years. The training for manhood begins. The boys are taught the needed skills to protect and provide for their tribe. They learn the unique history, stories and rituals of their ancestors. When the boys later return to the women, they have changed. They not only bear life-long scars on their bodies, they return to their tribe as new men. In one tribe, the mothers even pretend not to recognize their sons when they return.

Tribal cultures make sure that each and every boy is initiated into manhood. They include boys without fathers. The men make sure that no boys are left out.

Too many American boys fall through the cracks. They do not have a group of men to initiate them into manhood and support their growing independence from mothers. American boys often have far more women in their lives than men. Some have too much Mom and not enough Dad.

In schools, women teachers outnumber male teachers by six to one in K through 8[th,] grade and by two to one in high school. Women teachers can more naturally understand girl students. Some may not be as supportive of male nature and its physical aggressiveness and competitiveness. They may think it is odd that boys dog pile each other. (OK—it is odd!). Boys may be taught that any kind of aggression and fighting is wrong. But boys need validation that some kinds of fights are needed. Fighting evil is both good and necessary. We need police to protect us from criminals. We need a military to protect our country and allies from tyrants. Mothers and women can encourage boys to use their growing male strength constructively, and even to live by the warrior motto of the LAPD, "To Protect and to Serve." Every boy needs supportive and understanding moms and women in their lives.

Boys also desperately need supportive dads and men. Unfortunately, too many men and fathers are absent today. They left along the way. Nearly half of American boys will go to bed tonight without their biological father in the house. And many of those absent fathers left their sons before they were born. Four out of ten babies in the US are now born to unmarried mothers. There are millions of boys today who are missing their dads.

Boys without fathers grow up with an emotional ache in their hearts. The police chief of Detroit once said that the young men he arrests "not only don't have any responsible older man in the house — they have never met one. When you look at a gang, you are looking at young men who have no older men around them at all."[7] Over eighty percent of boys in gangs grow up without fathers. They turn to gang leaders to fill the void. This need to belong is the number one reason that boys join gangs. Dr. Steve Perry, founder and principal of Capital Preparatory Magnet School, has seen the pain in fatherless boys. "They don't know what to do with the anger," he says. "Every kid I've ever worked with who's been in a gang said they joined a gang for one reason. It's not protection. It's love."[8]

Boys find belonging in gangs but never learn the noble qualities of warriors to protect the innocent and uphold justice. In their pain and anger, they inflict violence upon each other. Boys may hope to learn courage and commitment from their gangs, but these positive qualities are perverted. "Courage" is used to hurt people and commit crime. That's not courage. It's cowardice. Uncontrolled aggression can lead to sexual assault on women. Boys without fathers have an overall higher risk to get hooked on drugs, drop out of school, and end up in jail. Going to prison can seem like a rite of passage.

Boys outside of gangs can also be adrift. Today's self-centered culture rarely teaches boys that a man's role is to protect others. Boys are not trained in the virtues of courage, self-control, or sacrifice for others. The historic warrior role of men is even frowned upon. Consequently, millions of boys play video games to initiate themselves as warriors. They spend billions of dollars on war games to fight like a warrior with cyber-courage and cyber-sacrifice. Their inner warrior longs to be challenged and tested. Unfortunately, many of these games are about violently killing innocent people. A true warrior doesn't do that—and doesn't enjoy that. That's flat out wrong. Be very careful with the video games you choose.

Other boys redefine "courage" to mean things like spouting profanity, bullying others, driving drunk, stealing and "scoring" sexually with as many women as possible. Without good men in their lives, they've never learned that courage is for doing good—not harm. The honorable qualities of a warrior fights for justice and does good to others. Boys need help to channel their male power to be constructive and protective. They need men to model these warrior qualities for them—not video games.

Warriors Shed their Blood for Others

The warrior men in the Kikuyu tribe in Kenya model an unmistakable commitment to their boys. They not only promise to shed their blood for their boys—they literally do it in their initiation rituals. As in other tribal rites of passage, they first take the boy away from his mother to a place outside the village. After three days of fasting, the boy is hungry and thirsty on the night of his initiation ceremony. Sitting around a fire with the men of the tribe, he watches as the oldest man takes out a knife, brightly reflected in the firelight. The man cuts open his own forearm and lets the blood flow down into a bowl on his lap. The knife and bowl are then passed around the circle—each man cutting himself and adding his blood to the bowl. When the bowl finally comes around the circle to the boy, he is given it to drink.[9]

In his childhood, a boy is nurtured by his mother's milk and her maternal care of him. This ritual teaches that men will also be committed and care for him. As a boy watches the men shed their blood with his own eyes, he will never forget their solidarity with him and their willingness to die for him in future warfare. He learns that manhood means courage, honor, self-control and the sacrifice of a warrior.

Warriors have self-control

Self-control is the hallmark of every disciplined warrior. Samurai warriors and martial arts practitioners don't just learn skills to subdue their enemy—they also learn to subdue and control themselves. As a warrior controls his aggression, so a man controls his anger. It is a cop-out to say you "lost" your temper. A man never loses his temper—he always chooses his temper.

Sometimes a man's worst enemy in life is himself. A man needs the self-control of a warrior to stop him from making stupid choices. Our world, however, often teaches men the opposite of self-control. One philosophy says, "If it feels good—just do it." This selfish and irresponsible way of living has ruined men's lives, marriages and families. A lack of sexual self-control has hurt countless women and left millions of children without fathers. A selfish life that indulges every impulse is completely normal for baby boys—but not for men.

The Bible teaches men to have self-control. In his letter to Titus, Paul describes the qualities older men need in order to mentor younger men. "Teach the older men to be temperate, worthy of respect, self-controlled, and sound in faith, in love, and in endurance....Similarly, encourage the young men to be self-controlled." (Titus 2:2, 6) As sexual desire and aggression are two of the strongest impulses in male nature, self-control is the key to channel these impulses to what is good.

Jesus: The Ultimate Warrior

The warrior traits of self-control and sacrifice are basic Christian qualities. Waging spiritual war until his death upon the cross, Jesus gives men the example of the ideal warrior of all time. He shed his blood on a cross to rescue us from death and give us eternal life.

At the end of his life, Jesus rode peacefully into Jerusalem on a colt. His return to earth will be as a warrior upon a horse. In the book of Revelation, John describes Jesus as a conquering warrior: "I saw heaven standing open and there before me was a white horse, whose rider is called Faithful and True. With justice he judges and makes war. His eyes are like blazing fire, and on his head are many crowns. He has a name written on him that no one knows but he himself. He is dressed in a robe dipped in blood and his name is the Word of God. The armies of heaven were following him, riding on white horses and dressed in fine linen, white and clean. Out of his mouth comes a sharp sword with which to strike down the nations. He will rule them with an iron scepter. He treads the winepress of the fury of the wrath of God Almighty. On his robe and on his thigh he has this name written: KING OF KINGS AND LORD OF LORDS." (Rev. 19:11-16) When Jesus returns, the world will see a warrior who comes to wage his final war on Satan. Jesus will triumph. Evil is vanquished forever.

Christian men follow a Warrior Lord who fights against injustice and evil. Start now to do the same in your life. Play fair against others. Don't cheat or lie. Defend others from bullies. Control your anger. Follow your Warrior Messiah into a manhood of courage, self-control and sacrifice for others.

A balanced Warrior may need to cry sometimes

After a battle, even the greatest warriors need to let down and cry sometimes. Men may be warriors but they still have hearts and feelings. If you have lost a friend or failed a test or your parents divorced—of course you feel pain. Don't deny that you are hurting inside. And never believe the old lie that "men don't cry." You need to share your tears and grief with someone. When hurting, you need to be comforted.

A balanced warrior knows he can be tough in some moments and tender in others. In anger Jesus turned over merchants' tables in the Temple. At his friend's grave, he felt the deepest grief and pain. The shortest verse in the Bible should be memorized by every warrior and man: "Jesus wept." (John 11:35)

Don't keep your fears or sad feelings to yourself. Let them out with people you trust. You will feel better every time. If you ever need to cry, then you need to cry. Talk it out with someone.

Jesus is committed to you

Jesus pounds on the door of every boy's life and with a loud voice calls him to "Come out!" Like the Kikuyu warriors, his commitment to boys is unmistakable. Jesus did not shed a small amount of his blood for others. He shed all of it. And he offers his own blood for every boy to drink.

The Eucharist cup will be passed around a fire on the night of your initiation ceremony. As you are served the Eucharist (or Communion), Jesus' own words are proclaimed again, "Unless you eat the flesh of the Son of Man and drink his blood, you have no life in you. Whoever eats my flesh and drinks my blood has eternal life, and I will raise him up at the last day. Whoever eats my flesh and drinks my blood remains in me, and I in him." (John 6:53-56) Christian boys have a commitment from a Warrior whose robe is dipped in blood and who laid down his life for them.

Tribal rituals train boys to become sacrificial warriors. The Crossing Rite of Passage also trains boys to become warriors, with Christ as their example. Always use your masculine strength and courage for the good. Protect others. Fight against evil, Satan's lies, a godless culture and your own self-centered desires. You will face many battles in life. Don't fight them alone. Get support from other men. Stir up your courage to "fight the good fight." Prepare yourself for war.

3

Christian Initiation Rituals

Like the blood-drinking ritual of African Kikuyu tribes, you will also be given blood to drink in your initiation into manhood. But this blood is not shed by either men or boys. In the cup of the Eucharist, the blood of Jesus himself will be offered for you to drink.

While the older Kikuyu men offer some of their blood to boys as a sign of their commitment, Jesus offered all of his blood. The ground under the cross was wet with his blood from his flogging, the thorns pounded into his head, the nails in his hands and feet, and from a spear thrust through his heart. He was a completely bloody sacrifice. Ultimately, a boy is initiated into Christian manhood not by other men, but by Jesus Himself.

Jesus left behind deeply meaningful sacraments for believers to remember him until he returns again someday. The sacraments express his grace and help to change our lives. They help transform boys from childhood into Christian manhood. Baptism, Confirmation of the Holy Spirit, and the Eucharist (Holy

Communion) are traditional Christian rituals that have transformed believers' lives for over two thousand years.

The Waters of Baptism

Water baptism makes believers clean. It washes away the old self to make a person new and born again. The runners in a mud run are a picture of how the old self looks both morally and spiritually to God. Baptism is a sacrament that washes away the mud.

Jewish believers also use baptism in their faith and practice. Long before John the Baptist came, Jews used ceremonial washings to purify those who had been defiled by anything "unclean". The washings symbolized cleansing from immoral acts. For centuries, the Mikvah, or ceremonial bath, has been practiced by Jews all over the world. Orthodox Jews enter into the Mikvah waters for a ceremonial bath every Friday afternoon before the start of the Sabbath.

The prophet Ezekiel wrote about the spiritual cleansing of baptism. As God spoke through Ezekiel, "I will sprinkle clean water on you, and you will be cleaned; I will cleanse you from all your impurities and from all your idols. I will give you a new heart and put a new spirit in you; I will remove from you your heart of stone and give you a heart of flesh." (Ezekiel 36:25-26) Christian baptism is a sacrament that also gives a new heart and spirit for those who believe in Christ.

Baptism also symbolizes identification with Jesus in his death and resurrection to a new life. As Paul wrote to the Roman church, "Don't you know that all of us who were baptized into Christ Jesus were baptized into his death? We were therefore buried with him through baptism into death." (Ro. 6:3-4) For believers in the first three centuries, this meant a literal death sentence. In the Roman Empire, baptism was a capital offense to the Caesars who believed that they alone were god. Countless Christians were executed for their faith, including many of the disciples. Peter was crucified upside down. Paul was beheaded.

Baptism was such a life-changing decision among early Christians that the Church made believers wait up to three years before they were baptized. This time of preparation included the study of Scripture, regular fasting and prayer, and growth in their faith. At the end of this time of initiation, most believers were baptized on Easter Sunday to further symbolize their spiritual resurrection with Christ.

Confirmation

After baptism in water, Christians in the early Church were anointed with oil to symbolize their baptism in the Holy Spirit. The sacrament of Confirmation with oil symbolically completed the baptism of the new believer. In the practice of the Old Testament, oil was used to anoint priests, kings and prophets. The name "Christ" literally means "the anointed one," the Greek translation for "Messiah". Confirmation was a ritual that anointed new believers as a "royal priesthood." (I Peter 2:9)

Chrism (from which we get Christ) is a mixture of olive oil and sweet-smelling balsam oil. After baptism, the priest anointed the new believer with this oil in the sign of the cross on his forehead (see Appendix for the signing prayer). Just as athletes in those times were anointed with oil before going into a contest, new Christians were also anointed for their life-long battle against Satan and the powers of evil. The priest then asked the new believer to publicly renounce Satan and all his works, followed by blowing on the believer to blow away Satan. The ceremony ended with the priest's blessing and putting salt on the believer's tongue, a symbol to be the salt of the earth.

After the anointing with oil, the priest made a traditionally Italian gesture. He lightly slapped the candidate on the cheek with his hand as an affectionate gesture of welcome into the faith. By the thirteenth century, the practice of striking the cheeks changed to also symbolize the suffering that Christians must endure from others.[10] As in tribal initiations that prepared boys for warfare, the anointing with oil and striking the cheek initiates boys to courageously face spiritual warfare in their lives.

The Eucharist

Hours before he was tortured and crucified, Jesus gave his disciples a profound way to remember him and his sacrifice forever. The sacrament of the Lord's Supper, or Eucharist (meaning Good Grace), brings us physically closer to Jesus by eating and drinking his body and blood. As Paul wrote, "The Lord Jesus, on the night he was betrayed, took bread, and when he had given thanks, he broke it and said, "This is my body, which is for you; do this in remembrance of me." In the same way, after supper he took the cup, saying, "This cup is the new covenant in my blood; do this, whenever you drink it, in remembrance of me." For whenever you eat this bread and drink this cup, you proclaim the Lord's death until he comes." (I Cor.11:23-26)

The Eucharist is a vivid reminder of Christ's love, sacrifice and commitment to believer's lives. It is also a reminder of how to live like Christ. As Jesus told his disciples, "My command is this: Love each other as I have loved you. Greater love has no one than this, that he lay down his life for his friends." (John 15:12-13) The central quality of Christian life and Christian manhood is to love others with the same kind of commitment and sacrifice.

The Sacraments in the Crossing into Manhood Ceremony

The Christian sacraments of the Eucharist and anointing with oil will be used in your rite of passage ceremony. (If you are not already baptized and you feel ready for this sacrament, talk with your pastor or Mentor Team to take this step too). During the Mentor Team initiation ceremony around a campfire, the mentors will mark your forehead with oil in the sign of the cross to anoint you into the grace of the Christian life. The body and blood of Christ will also be served to you in the Eucharist cup and bread. Salt will be placed on your tongue. Mentor Team lessons will be reviewed. Lastly, the men will bless you with words of wisdom, Scripture, prayers, and special gifts.

Jesus left behind some powerful rituals to connect us to him. They help us experience his love and grace. In your new life as a young man, remember that God deeply loves you. Receive his love for you every day. Whenever you fall, God will always pick you up. Whenever you sin, confess and repent and he will forgive and make you clean. God is your best ally. His sacraments will help you to never forget.

5

Lessons in Manhood

Crossing from Boyhood to Manhood

10 Minutes

I. Introductions: Getting to Know your Mentor Team and Brothers

Write down the names, ages and birthdays of the Men and Boys in your team. Share about your favorite superhero.

<u>Mentor Team</u>

Name   Birthday   Favorite Superhero

<u>Boys/Young Men</u>

Name   Birthday   Favorite Superhero

30 Minutes
II. Manhood is Your Destiny: Saying Goodbye to Boyhood

Assign a Mentor to read:

Childhood is not meant to last into your twenties, thirties or beyond. There is a time to be a boy and a time to be a man. Now is your time to become a man. Manhood has been your destiny since you were born. But like Peter Pan, some men never want to grow up. They live irresponsible and self-centered lives, and these men, along with their wives and children suffer from it. God has something better for you and your future wife and children. Boyhood is great, but a God-centered manhood is even greater. Crossing from boyhood into manhood is the best choice you will ever make.

III. Rites of Passage help Boys become Men

Assign a boy to read:

Boys don't become men just by growing older. They need ritual and mentoring to become men. A Rite of Passage prepares boys to become men of character, courage and wisdom. Just as athletes need coaching to become successful in their sport, boys need coaching to become successful men. This rite of passage is your own spring training for manhood. Your Mentor Team will coach you with Lessons in Manhood, rituals and experiences that will help you become a man.

A. The Crossing Rite of Passage from Boyhood into Manhood.

Review the Rite of Passage and Training Calendar on page 15. Write down some estimated dates for the various lessons and events. Add some creative ideas from your team.

Review these other rites of passage into manhood:

B. The Jewish Bar Mitzvah: Transforming Boys into Godly Men

Bar Mitzvah means "Son of the Commandment." Every Jewish boy becomes a Bar Mitzvah on his 13th birthday—with or without a ceremony. Upon turning 13, the new young man becomes responsible to obey God's commandments. The Bible has 613 mitzvoth (commandments), including the two greatest commands to love God and to love others.

Discussion Question:

What are some responsibilities of Jewish boys in their Bar Mitzvah ceremony?

C. Tribal Rites of Passage: Transforming Boys into Warrior Men

Warriors are trained to protect their tribe, country, women and children. Refer to Chapter One for the following discussion.

Discussion Questions:

What are some rituals used in tribal initiations to prepare boys for war?

Why are they so painful and bloody?

D. Modern Rites of Passage: Turning Boys into Men...or just Older Boys?

Most modern day "rites of passage" do not require any character changes or sacrifice. They are mostly meaningless. Only a few are honorable.

Discuss:

When do boys become adult men in today's culture?

When can they legally smoke, drink alcohol, go to bars, strip clubs, and casinos?

What character qualities, if any, do these "adult" acts require?

What ages can men drive, work, vote and serve in the military?

What character qualities do the above responsibilities require?

What are some honorable and older definitions of manhood in our nation's culture and history?

25 Minutes

IV. Growing in Wisdom and Stature: The Example of Christ

Jesus is the model for all Christian men. He shows us how to live, love, think, and serve both God and others. The Bible teaches us to continually grow and mature throughout our lives. Jesus himself grew in wisdom from the time he was twelve years old.

Assign two boys to read about growth as a man.

"When I was a child I talked like a child, I thought like a child, and I reasoned like a child. When I became a man, I put childish ways behind me." I Cor. 13:11

"And Jesus grew in wisdom and in stature." Luke 2:52 (a description of Jesus after the age of twelve)

Assign a Mentor to read:

Wisdom is a key to mature manhood. Wise choices will make you successful in your life and relationships. Foolish choices can lead you to destruction. Jesus didn't just grow bigger, he became wiser. A man can grow up to be 6'10" and 250 lbs but not grow an inch in wisdom. Whatever your height becomes, make sure to grow in wisdom for the rest of your life. Proverbs says that reverence for the Lord is the beginning of wisdom, "but fools despise wisdom and instruction." (Proverbs 1:7). Wisdom comes from knowing God's heart and following his instruction.

Discussion:

Think of some men that are successful in sports or entertainment, but destroyed their lives with foolish choices. What choices ruined their lives?

Have one of the Mentors give an example of how wisdom helped him to make a better choice over foolishness.

What are some wise and foolish choices that teens face today?

Follow Jesus' Example: Grow in Wisdom

Four Sources of Wisdom

1. Read God's Word. Read the Bible as often as you can. It will guide your steps and choices in life.

2. Connect with godly men and women. Learn from their lives and wisdom.

3. Ask God for wisdom and He will generously give it to you.

4. Learn from your experiences—both good and bad, successes and failures. Build upon the good, receive grace for the bad. Try again.

VI. Wrap Up & Homework

Turn to the One Year Training Calendar on page 17 and write in today's date for today's lesson.

Memorize Luke 2:52 "And Jesus grew in wisdom and in stature."

Close with Prayer.

Read Proverbs chapters 1-5. What are three benefits of having wisdom?

1.

2.

3.

Read the next Lesson on Jesus: The Model for Manhood.

Lessons in Manhood   Number Two

Jesus:
The Model for Manhood

We can model our lives after good examples or bad examples of men. Follow good examples and your life will be infinitely better. This lesson explores the greatest example of manhood of all time.

10 Minutes

I. Examples of Great Men

Name some of the greatest men who ever lived, whether alive today or in the past. Write a list of at least ten men.

1.   6.

2.   7.

3.   8.

4.   9.

5.   10.

Write at least ten character qualities of the above men on your team's list.

1.   6.

2.   7.

3.   8.

4.   9.

5.   10.

20 Minutes

II. The Ideal Model of Manhood: Jesus the Son of God

As the first man, Adam could have been our perfect model of manhood. But Adam and Eve had a problem with authority, just as we do, and they ruined their potential example for us. Every human since has not been a perfect example. We all fall short. As the Son of God and Son of Man, Jesus is our perfect example. We will never be perfect like him because of our human nature, but we can grow to become more like him every day. Jesus said, "I am the Way, the Truth and the Life."(John 14:6) As he said to the disciples, he also says to you, "Follow me."

List ten or more character qualities of Jesus with your team

1.   6.

2.   7.

3.   8.

4.   9.

5.   10.

How do Jesus' character qualities compare with your list of great men and their qualities?

What are three of Jesus' character qualities that you most admire? Circle them above.

Paul and Peter spell out more Christian qualities. Read these two Scriptures and list the qualities here:

Galatians 5:22	II Peter 1:5-8
"The Fruit of the Spirit is…"	"Make every effort to add to your faith…"

1.   1.

2.   2.

3.   3.

4.   4.

5.   5.

6.   6.

7.   7.

8.

III. Imitating Christ

Paul teaches us to be like Christ. Assign three boys to read these Scriptures:

"Your attitude should be the same as that of Christ Jesus" (Phil. 2:5)

"Be imitators of God…and live a life of love, just as Christ loved us." (Eph.5:1)

"For those God foreknew he also predestined to be conformed to the likeness of his Son, that he might be the firstborn of many brothers." Romans 8:29

As a boy, your destiny is manhood. As a Christian, you are predestined to be like Christ.

15 Minutes

III. How Character makes life better

Discuss how Christian character qualities make a positive difference in your life. Give examples of how these qualities can help you succeed in the following areas.

Friendships.

The friends you choose.

Sports.

School.

Family life.

Relations with girls.

Work and daily chores.

Staying away from crime and prison.

Staying away from drugs and alcohol.

Waiting to have a baby until after marriage.

IV. Wrap Up & Homework

Christian manhood means daily growth in character and imitating Christ.

Memorize Galatians 5:22. "The fruit of the Spirit is love, joy, peace, patience, kindness, goodness, faithfulness, gentleness and self-control."

Close with Prayer.

Read the next Lesson on Manhood with a Mission.

NOTES

Lessons in Manhood   Number Three

Manhood with a Mission and Code of Honor

15 Minutes

I. Your Life has a Mission

Assign a Mentor to read:

You have a mission to change the world for good. Every adventure movie, disaster movie or super hero movie is a story about the Good overcoming the Bad. Mission Impossible, James Bond, The Lord of the Rings, and every super hero movie from Spider-Man to Iron Man—all have a mission to triumph over evil and save the world. Your mission is the same. But your mission is neither a movie nor fiction. It's real. Christian men are called to be revolutionaries to help bring the world back to God's original design. The world has been in bad shape since Adam. You can help make it better again. This lesson will help clarify your mission in life and give you a code of honor to live by.

II. Missions Shape our Actions

Assign a boy to read:

Missions give direction, goals, and purpose in life; usually to help someone else or to make the world a better place. A mission to follow Christ, be a committed father, or to build water wells in Nigeria are examples of missions. Military and space programs are also called missions. Military missions fight battles against our enemies. Space missions will land people on Mars someday.

Name the mission of the following:

1. The U.S. Military in WWII

2. Your local police department

3. Frodo and Sam in The Lord of the Rings

4. Major League Baseball Teams

5. Olympic Athletes

6. Middle School and High School Students

7. Jesus

10 Minutes

III. The Mission of Christian Men

You have a mission to bring God's light and love into a dark and hurting world. Jesus said to "let your light so shine before men, that they may see your good works and glorify your Father in heaven." He also said, "Go and make disciples." Spread the good news. Tell your story to others. Let people know how Christ changed your life. Comfort others in need. Overcome evil with good.

Give some practical examples of how you have touched or served others with God's love. Even little acts like giving someone a cup of water count in God's eyes.

Examples of Christian service.

25 Minutes
IV. Living by a Code of Honor

Examples of Codes of Honor

Men have lived by codes of honor for thousands of years. A code of honor is a code of conduct that shapes how you behave and treat others. A code influences our choices. It states our values. This exercise will have you write your own code of honor. To get started, read aloud the codes of honor on the following pages. Then write you own code of honor on the worksheet at the end.

Chivalry code of honor

Samurai code of honor

Tae Kwon Do code of honor

US Military codes of honor

Judeo-Christian code of honor/Ten Commandments

Medieval English Chivalry Code of Conduct

- Live to defend Crown and Country and all it holds dear.
- Live one's life so that it is worthy of respect and honor.
- Live for freedom, justice and all that is good.
- Never attack an unarmed foe.
- Never attack from behind.
- Avoid lying to your fellow man.
- Avoid cheating.
- Obey the law of king, country, and chivalry.
- Administer justice.
- Protect the innocent.
- Respect women.
- Exhibit self control.
- Exhibit courage in word and deed.
- Defend the weak and innocent.
- Destroy evil in all of its monstrous forms.
- Crush the monsters that steal our land and rob our people.
- Fight with honor.
- Never abandon a friend, ally, or noble cause.
- Never betray a confidence or comrade.
- Die with valor.

Samurai Bushido Code of Honor
"The Way of the Warrior"

- Justice: Doing the right thing.

- Courage: Being brave and heroic

- Mercy: Caring for those in need

- Respect: Treating others with politeness and dignity

- Honesty: Being truthful

- Honor: Your reputation as worthy of honor

- Loyalty: Faithful and devoted

- Self-Control: Choosing right over wrong

The Tae Kwon Do Code of Honor

- Be loyal to your country

- Be loving and show fidelity to your parents

- Be loving between husband and wife

- Be cooperative between brothers and sisters

- Be faithful to your friends

- Be respectful to your elders.

- Establish trust between teacher and student.

- Use good judgment before killing any living thing.

- Never retreat in battle.

- Always finish what you start.

West Point Military Academy Cadet Code of Honor

"A cadet will not lie, cheat, steal, or tolerate those who do."

United States Armed Forces Mottos

U.S. Marines:	Semper Fidelis. "Always Faithful"
U.S. Army:	"This We'll Defend"
U.S. Navy:	Non sibi sed patriae. "Not Self, But Country"
U.S. Air Force:	"Aim High...Fly, Fight, Win"
U.S. Coast Guard	Semper Paratus. "Always Ready"

United States Fighting Forces Code of Honor

I. I am an American fighting in the forces which guard my country and our way of life. I am prepared to give my life in their defense...and to oppose the enemies of the United States and support its national interests.

II. I will never surrender of my own free will. If in command, I will never surrender the members of my command while they still have the means to resist.

III. If I am captured I will continue to resist by all means available. I will make every effort to escape and aid others to escape. I will accept neither parole nor special favors from the enemy.

IV. If I become a prisoner of war, I will keep faith with my fellow prisoners. I will give no information nor take part in any action which might be harmful to my comrades.

V. When questioned, should I become a prisoner of war, I am required to give name, rank, service number, and date of birth. I will evade answering further questions to the utmost of my ability. I will make no oral or written statements disloyal to my country and its allies or harmful to their cause.

VI. I will never forget that I am an American, fighting for freedom, responsible for my actions, and dedicated to the principles which made my country free. I will trust in my God and in the United States of America.

The life of a prisoner of war is hard. Each person in this stressful situation must always sustain hope and resist enemy indoctrination. Prisoners of war standing firm and united against the enemy will support and inspire one another in surviving their ordeal and in prevailing over misfortune with honor.

Judeo-Christian Code of Conduct

The Ten Commandments

1   You shall have no other gods before me.

2   You shall not make for yourself an idol...or bow down to them.

3   You shall not misuse the name of the Lord your God.

4   Remember the Sabbath day by keeping it holy.

5   Honor your father and your mother.

6   You shall not murder.

7   You shall not commit adultery.

8   You shall not steal.

9   You shall not lie.

10 You shall not covet your neighbor's house, wife, servants or anything that belongs to him.

Exodus 20

My Personal Code of Honor

Your code of honor is your personal code of conduct. It guides the choices you make and how you live and relate to others. Some examples of Christian conduct include love, patience, goodness, kindness, and self-control. To help you remember just three of these, circle three character qualities from the following list (or add other qualities) that are personally meaningful to you and write your own three-word code of honor.

Honesty	Loyalty
Integrity	Respect
Courage	Discipline
Self-Control	Commitment
Love	Patience
Kindness	Humility
Goodness	Thankful
Generosity	Forgiveness
Faithful	Gracefulness
Perseverance	Compassion

My Code of Honor:

_____, _____, _____,

Discuss why you chose your code. Think of some examples of how you can live by this code.

5 Minutes
IV. Wrap Up & Homework

You have a great mission in life—to spread God's love and make the world a better place.

Frame Your Code of Honor

After you have chosen your personal Code of Honor, print it out on a printer and frame it. Bring it to your next Mentor Team Lesson to show the others. Then hang it on your wall as a reminder to yourself from now through the end of high school. Live by it daily. And whenever you fail, remember God's grace is always there to forgive and to pick you back up again. Even Peter blew it sometimes. But just as God was gracious to him, God is also gracious to you. When you see your Code of Honor, also remember that you have been saved by grace—not by works, and not by this Code. Your Code is a simple reminder of some Christian qualities to live by.

Memorize the Ten Commandments.
You can't obey them if you don't know them.

Read the next Lesson on The Manhood of a King

Close with a Prayer

Lessons in Manhood   Number Four

The Manhood of a King:
to Bless and to Serve

20 Minutes

I. Two Kinds of Kings—Two Kinds of Power

Like good or bad kings, men can use their masculine power either constructively or destructively. Male power can build people up or tear people down. A good king is a servant leader, using his power to serve and bless his people and kingdom. A tyrant king abuses his power by oppressing people for his own selfish gain.

Give examples of the two kinds of kings; whether living today or in history, books or movies. Also describe their character qualities.

Tyrant Kings   Qualities

1.

2.

3.

Good Kings   Qualities

1.

2.

3.

Modern "Kings"

As many countries no longer have kings today, who are some men in leadership positions with power in government, business, technology, entertainment or sports? Do they use their leadership to serve others or to only serve themselves?

1.

2.

3.

Who are some men who have power and authority in your life, such as fathers, teachers, coaches and pastors? Do they use their leadership to serve others or to only serve themselves?

1.

2.

3.

II. The King of Kings and Lord of Lords

The Bible recognizes Jesus as "the King of Kings and Lord of Lords." And Jesus himself states that "All authority in heaven and on earth has been given to me."(Mt.28:18) His power is unlimited. Yet he uses his power to empower others—not to make them feel powerless or small. As a King, he shows us how to use power to bless and to serve people.

10 Minutes
III. A Good King Blesses Others

A. Examples of Blessings

Assign three boys to read the next three points:

The Hebrew word for blessing is "to kneel". It shows respect and value to others. A good king blesses people with words and actions. He doesn't use his power for his own sake and ego. He is concerned about others' needs. We bless others by saying encouraging words and being good to them.

1. Jewish Kings blessed their kingdom and descendents

Blessing others is an ancient kingly tradition in Jewish history, including David blessing his son Solomon before he died, saying, "So be strong, show yourself a man, and observe what the Lord your God requires." (I Kings 2:2) Earlier Isaac blessed Jacob (Gen 27:27), and Jacob blessed Joseph and his grandsons, saying,

"Bring them to me so I may bless them." So Joseph brought his sons close to him, and his father kissed them and

65

embraced them...then he blessed Joseph and said, "May the God before whom my fathers Abraham and Isaac walked...bless these boys...and may they increase greatly upon the earth." (Gen. 48)

Fathers asked God to bless their sons with more children and wealth than they had. They are happy for their children to be more successful than themselves.

2.   Jewish parents bless their children

Blessings are also practiced by Jewish parents throughout the ages. Every Friday night before the Sabbath dinner, Jewish parents go around their table, put their hands on the children's heads and bless them.

3.   Jesus blessed children.

"People were bringing little children to Jesus to have him touch them...And he took the children in his arms, put his hands on them and blessed them." (Mark 10:13)

B. How to Bless Others

The biblical practice of blessing includes a touch (a hand on the head or shoulder), a spoken word, and a commitment. Show your respect and care for others by verbalizing encouraging words. Pray for others' needs (either with them or by yourself). If they are receptive, greet and bless them with a handshake, hand on their shoulder, hug or pat on the back. Let them know you will also be there for them.

15 Minutes
III. A Good King Serves Others: True Greatness

Assign two Mentors to read A and B:

A. A New Definition of Greatness

When the disciples John and James asked to be at Jesus' right and left hand in his kingdom, Jesus taught them a new definition of power and greatness.

"Jesus called them together and said, "You know that those who are regarded as rulers of the Gentiles lord it over them, and their high officials exercise authority over them. Not so with you. Instead, whoever wants to become great among you must be your servant. For even the Son of Man did not come to be served, but to serve." Mark 10:42-45

Be a great man by serving others. True greatness gives instead of takes.

B. Jesus' Example of Service with Humility.

Washing another person's feet was only done by slaves in Jesus' time. But even that act of humble service was not beneath the King of Kings.

"Jesus knew that the Father had put all things under his power...so he got up from the meal, took off his outer clothing, and wrapped a towel around his waist. After that he poured water into a basin and began to wash his disciples' feet, drying them with the towel that was wrapped around his waist...When he had finished washing their feet, he put on his clothes and returned to his place. "Do you understand what I have done for you?" he asked them. "Now that I, your Lord and Teacher have washed your feet, you also should wash one another's feet. I have set you an example that you should do as I have done for you. I tell you the truth, no servant is greater than his master...Now that you know these things, you will be blessed if you do them." (John 13:3-5,12-17)

Discussion.

How you can apply this example of a servant leader in your life? What are some practical ways you can serve others in your family, school, church and community? Write at least five here. You might choose one of these for your Good Deeds Project.

1.

2.

3.

4.

5.

5 Minutes
IV. Wrap Up & Homework

Be a great young man. Act like a good king and servant leader. Serve others this week.

Bless someone. Think of how you can bless people around you this week, at least one person each day. Ask someone how they are doing, give an encouraging word or compliment, give a pat on the back. Make someone's day.

Serve Someone. Do an act of service this week in your family, school, church or anywhere else. Even little acts can mean a lot to people. As Jesus said, "You will be blessed if you do them." (John 13:17) Be a *great* man. Serve somebody.

Memorize. "Whoever wants to be great among you must be your servant." (Mark 10:43)

Read the next Lesson on The Manhood of a Warrior.

Close with a Prayer.

NOTES

Lessons in Manhood   Number Five

The Manhood of a Warrior: To Protect and Fight

10 Minutes
I. Tribal Initiations Transform Boys into Warriors

What are some tribal rituals that train boys for war? Why all the pain and blood?

10 Minutes
II. The Warrior Nature of Men

Assign two Mentors to read A and B.

A. Warriors and Male Body Strength.

Men have been responsible to protect women and children since time began. The simple reason for this role is because men's body size and strength are greater than women's. Men have nearly 50% more upper body strength than women and 30% more aerobic capacity for endurance. This greater strength is one reason why men make up 85% of our military and 87% of police. 24% of all American men are veterans, while 2% are women. The motto of the LAPD, "To Protect and to Serve," applies to every man. Your role is to protect and defend others—not to physically or verbally hurt others. Stand up straight and you will feel and act stronger.

B. Warriors and Male Hormones.

Testosterone is like fuel. This hormone fuels male aggression, competition and sexual drive. Men have 20 times the amount of this hormone than women. The peak years of men's testosterone level are in the late teens and twenties. These are not only the peak fighting ages of men in tribes or military, these are also the peak ages for the sex drive which leads to marriage and children. This time of added strength adds to men's courage to face all kinds of fears and foes in life. Most revolutions are started by youth. Most of Jesus' own disciples were in their twenties.

Men must channel and control their aggressive nature. A man trained in the martial arts uses self-control to stay out of fights—not to start them. Learn to control your emotions and aggression. Remember that you never lose your temper—you always choose your temper.

20 Minutes
II. Fighting Good Fights

A. The Good Fight of Competition

Assign Mentors & Boys to read and discuss:

Men don't just fight on battlefields. Think of some common chants in football games against opposing teams. What kind of words are used?

Sports are a kind of war on the court, turf or pitch. But men also compete in business, school, medicine and everywhere else in life. The male drive to compete pushes men to excel. The status quo is never good enough. Something can always be done better. Technology is always improved. Someday there will be an iPhone 70. Olympic records will always be broken. The warrior nature in men leads to advancements in every field. Competition is good — but remember to lighten up, relax and take a break sometimes. Stay balanced!

Give some examples of great rivalries in:

Sports:

Technology companies:

Your local schools:

B. The Good Fight to Defend Others.

When under self-control, the warrior nature of men is protective and defends the weak. Good Warriors confront evil and injustice. The warrior Moses modeled this when he confronted Pharaoh face to face and demanded, "Let my people go!" Warriors risk their lives for others. Over 290,000 American soldiers died while fighting evil in Europe and Asia in World War II. Without good warriors, our world would be overrun by evil. As Edmund Burke wrote, "The only thing necessary for the triumph of evil is for good men to do nothing."

Corrupt men can be found in politics, business, sports, and even in a church. Men who use their male strength to physically harm innocents are bullies and thugs—not warriors. Gangbangers and criminals dishonor their manhood. Proverbs says to stay away from these men. "Do not give in to them. If they say, "Come along with us; let's lie in wait for someone's blood, let's waylay some harmless soul...we will get all sorts of valuable things and fill our houses with plunder; my son, do not go along with them, do not set foot on their paths." (Proverbs 1:10-15)

Discuss some examples of heroic men who have confronted evil.

C. The Good Fight of the Faith

Before Paul was executed for being a Christian, he wrote these final words to Timothy, "The time has come for my departure, I have fought the good fight, I have finished the race, I have kept the faith." He then challenged Timothy to do the same, "Fight the good fight of the faith." (I Tim. 4:6-7, 6:12)

15 Minutes
III. Three Fights of Christian Men

Assign three Mentors to read A,B,C.

A. Enemy Number One: Satan (The Accuser)

Don't be deceived by this invisible enemy. He shows up in many places and temptations. His intention is always to destroy you. "Be self-controlled and alert. Your enemy the devil prowls around like a roaring lion looking for someone to devour. Resist him, standing firm in the faith." (I Peter 4:8-9) Self-control will help save you from his temptations. Stand firm in your faith. As Paul reassures you, "The God of peace will soon crush Satan under your feet." (Romans 16:20)

The devil "showed Jesus all the kingdoms of the world and their splendor. "All this I will give you," he said, "if you will bow down and worship me." Jesus said to him, "Away from me, Satan! For it is written, "Worship the Lord your God, and serve Him only." (Mt. 4:8-10) Jesus fought Satan's lies and temptations with the truth of Scripture.

What are some common temptations or acts of Satan today that men must fight?

B. Enemy Number Two: The World

Jesus said, "All men will hate you because of me." (Mt. 10:22) He also said, "If the world hates you, keep in mind that it hated me first. If you belonged to the world, it would love you as its own. As it is, you do not belong to the world, but I have chosen you out of the world. That is why the world hates you...If they persecuted me, they will persecute you also." (John 15:18-20)

The world tempts us to turn away from God. It promotes selfishness and godlessness. John wrote, "Do not love the world or anything in the world...For everything in the world—the cravings of sinful man, the lust of his eyes and the boasting of what he has and does—comes not from the Father but from the world." (I John 2:15-16)

While you don't live like the world lives, you have a mission to help restore the world. Jesus said, "I am the light of the world." (John 8:12) He says the same to you, "You are the light of the world." (Mt. 5:14) "For God so loved the world that he gave his one and only Son, that whoever believes in him shall not perish but have eternal life. For God did not send his Son into the world to condemn the world, but to save the world through him." (John 3:16-17). Have a heart for the world just as God cares for the world.

Protect yourself from the ways of this world, but also share God's light and love to touch people in the world.

What are some common temptations of the world that men need to fight?

C. Enemy Number Three: Your own human nature

Paul wrote about the battle within himself between his sinful nature and his Spirit. "So I say, live by the Spirit, and you will not gratify the desires of the sinful nature. For the sinful nature desires what is contrary to the Spirit, and the Spirit what is contrary to the sinful nature. They are in conflict with each other, so that you do not do what you want... The acts of the sinful nature are obvious; sexual immorality, impurity and debauchery, idolatry and witchcraft, hatred, discord, jealousy, fit of rage, selfish ambition, dissensions, factions and envy; drunkenness, orgies and the like." (Gal.5:16-23)

What are some common temptations of your human nature that you often need to fight?

10 Minutes
IV. Winning the Fight

A.   Pray and read God's Word

B.   Live by Your Code of Honor

C.   Use Self-Control

D.   Have a band of brothers for support. Regularly talk with trusted friends. Don't be a loner.

E.   Remember Jesus' example of fighting to the end. "If anyone would come after me, he must deny himself and take up his cross and follow me." (Mt. 16:24)

V. When You Lose—Get Back Up

Warriors don't win every battle. Like Peter, even those with the strongest convictions to die for their faith can fail. Peter denied he even knew Jesus three times. But even though Peter miserably failed, Jesus forgave him and restored him. As he earlier told Peter, "Simon, Simon, Satan has asked to sift you as wheat. But I have prayed for you, Simon, that your faith may not fail. And when you have turned back, strengthen your brothers."
(Luke 22:31)

When you fail any battles, always turn back. Get back up. Don't give up. God's grace is greater than your failure. Receive His forgiveness. Try again. Get back in the fight.

10 Minutes
VI. Balanced Warriors

Warriors have feelings too. The old saying that "men don't cry" is not true. Everyone has grief, fears and pain at times. "There is a time to weep and a time to laugh." (Eccl. 3:4) We need to talk and find comfort from others when we grieve. Grief needs to be shared—not stuffed inside.

What is the shortest verse in the Bible? Write it here:

How do you feel about crying when you are hurting?

Who can you talk to for support in times of temptation, fears, failure or grief?

VII. Wrap Up & Homework

Protect and Serve. Who can you protect, serve or defend this week? What are some practical examples within your family, school, friends or community?

Memorize I Timothy 6:12: "Fight the good fight of the faith."

Close with a prayer.

Read the next Lesson on Manhood with Care and Respect for Women.

Lesson in Manhood   Number Six

Manhood with Care
and Respect for Women

Assign a Mentor to read:

God made us in His image, both male and female. We are
perfectly equal and perfectly made for each other. Thank God for
making women! They are your sisters, mothers and aunts,
teachers and co-workers, as well as classmates and friends. Value
them all.

You may or may not have physical attractions to girls at your
present age, but most boys will develop strong desires for girls by
the age of sixteen. These attractions are something to both enjoy
and control for a lifetime. This lesson talks about why boys have
attractions to the opposite sex and how to treat women with care
and respect. Also included is some useful information about the
changes that happen to the male body in the teenage years.

10 Minutes

I.   Three Reasons for our Attractions to Women

Assign three boys to read each reason.

A. For companionship. To have a wife someday

The Lord God said, "It is not good for the man to be alone. I will
make a helper suitable for him....Then the Lord God made a

woman from the rib he had taken out of the man, and he brought her to the man….For this reason a man will leave his father and his mother and be united to his wife, and they will become one flesh. The man and his wife were both naked, and they felt no shame" (Genesis 2:18, 22)

After making the world and everything in it, "God saw all that He had made, and it was very good." (Gen. 1:31)

What was the first thing in the world that God saw was *not* good?

Your attractions to girls and their friendship are God-given and good. God created us male and female for companionship and marriage.

B. To have children

God blessed Adam and Eve and said to them, "Be fruitful and increase in number." (Gen.1:28) Having children is the greatest blessing for a man. After marriage you can become a father and raise children with your wife. Marriage first—then children.

Why is it best to be married before having children?

C. To enjoy her beauty

King Solomon wrote a whole book about his attractions to his bride's beauty. In The Song of Songs, he says: "How beautiful you are my darling! Oh, how beautiful! Your eyes are doves.

Your lips are like a scarlet ribbon; your mouth is lovely. Your two breasts are like two fawns. You have stolen my heart with one glance of your eyes." (verses from the Song of Songs)

Who are some girls in movies or music artists that you think are beautiful?

What are some other qualities you find attractive in girls?

15 Minutes
II. Why Attractions need Self-Control

Assign a Mentor to read:

As with all of our human passions, we also need to control our attractions for girls and their beauty. Sexual desires can feel as powerful as riding a horse. Yet even small jockeys can control the strongest of horses. Practice self-control. Your desires for girls are good. But they are not good if you use a girl only for pleasure — without commitment, responsibility or care for her.

King David acted on his sexual desires without any self-control, respect or responsibility for Bathsheba. He abused his power as a man and a king, used her and raped her.

"One evening David got up from his bed and walked around on

the roof of the palace. From the roof he saw a woman bathing. The woman was very beautiful. She was Bathsheba, the wife of Uriah. Then David sent messengers to get her. She came to him, and he slept with her. Then the woman went back home. The woman conceived and sent word to David, saying, "I am pregnant." 2 Sam. 11

A similar temptation for men and boys today is to lust after women in pornography. The average age that boys first see pornography on the internet is eleven. Although looking at porn does not rape a woman like David raped Bathsheba, it stirs up a similar sexual desire, without any care for her as a person. Be very careful to control yourself when tempted to look at porn. Because the male brain is so visually stimulated by women, men and boys can become addicted to pornography like a drug.

You have much better things to do with your time. The more control you have now over pornography will help you have more control later in your life. Paul said, "Flee from porneia." (I Corinthians 6:18). "Porneia" is the Greek word for sexual immorality. Paul also said, "I will not be mastered by anything." (I Cor.6:12) We should not be mastered by food, porn, alcohol, drugs, video games or anything else. We are meant to be free. Don't be ashamed to ever ask for help or to talk to someone about your temptations. Turn to a trusted friend for support if you ever feel mastered by porn or anything else.

Remember that your desires for girls are good, but they require responsibility, self-control and respect. Your desires will ultimately be channeled to your wife someday. Be patient and self-controlled until then. You will have a lifetime of pleasure with your wife once you are married someday.

5 Minutes
III. Loving like a Good King: To Bless and to Serve

Assign a Mentor to read III and IV.

When you love a girl someday, remember to treat her with the care and manhood of a good king. Start now with how you treat your mother, sisters, and other girls. Bless them and be considerate of their needs. Be respectful and helpful. Treat them with honor. Be a good listener. Open doors for them. Let them to go first. Walk with them when alone in the dark.

What are some other ways to treat girls well? Write here:

What are some ways you have seen men not treat women well?

5 Minutes
IV. Loving like a Warrior: To Protect and Defend

Paul says that love "always protects." (I Cor 13:7) When you love a girl someday, treat her with the protective care of a good warrior. Start now by controlling your language, words or profanities around girls. Control your anger. Be patient. Be considerate of their safety and security. And never, never, never touch her body against her will. If she says or looks like she doesn't want you to touch her—don't.

What are some other ways to protect and defend girls?

10 Minutes

V. Mothers' Advice on How to Treat Girls

Have a Mentor read the list that was collected from the mothers and other women on how to treat girls with care and respect. The boys will write down the answers in their books.

What are the main character qualities that women want in a man?

Mother's Advice Continued.

What are some practical ways that boys can treat girls well?

10 Minutes
VI. Growing into a Man's Body

Assign a Mentor to Read:

Puberty is the time period, ages 11-17, when a boy's body changes into an adult man's body. Though you've had a penis since you were born, your body will now grow in these secondary sexual characteristics: erections at night when asleep, in the morning when you wake (called "the morning wood") and nearly any time of day during puberty, which can be pretty awkward during school. During sleep or if you masturbate, your penis will ejaculate semen (the liquid that carries your sperm that can fertilize a woman's egg). Other changes include pubic hair, facial hair, deeper voice and more muscles, height and weight. Before puberty, most boys are an inch shorter than girls. By 17, most boys are 5 inches taller. Testosterone is the hormone that fuels all these changes in boys. It makes boys more aggressive, competitive, and sexually attracted to girls.

The estrogen hormone in girls changes their bodies to make them taller, develop breasts, and prepare their womb for pregnancy if their egg is fertilized by sperm. They will start having periods around ages 11-13—a monthly bloody menstruation which flushes out the womb to prepare for the next month's egg. A girl's body will ovulate about twelve eggs per year.

Puberty will make your testicles bigger to start producing sperm, which makes it possible to have a baby with a girl. Each ejaculation of a boy has over 200 million sperm. But even though you are physically able to become a father, you are nowhere near ready to be one. Self-control will help you postpone sexual intercourse until you are married. Save that one act of sexual intimacy until marriage. There are many other ways to be affectionate with a girlfriend or fiancé without having intercourse.

Your body is about to go through some amazing changes. Your penis will become more active than ever before. If you ever masturbate—always keep it alone and in private. It's not a shameful thing if you ever pleasure yourself. Don't heap guilt on yourself. But as Paul wrote about any pleasures, don't be mastered by it either. You have better things to do with your time. As in most things in life, self-control and moderation is needed over any of our bodily pleasures. Get to know and take care of your new and changing body. Stay healthy. And as you become a man physically, keep growing as a man spiritually too.

VII.   Stay Connected

You don't have to walk alone through this journey with your growing body and attractions to girls. Think of older men that you can talk to along the way; your father, brother, Mentor Team member, or anyone else you can trust. Also think of an older woman that you trust who can help you understand girls.

• as your body grows and changes, ask questions you may have.

• as you develop feelings and attractions for girls, you may be excited or afraid, happy or sad, bold or shy. Talking to someone you trust can help you cope with all these normal feelings and help you understand and better relate to girls.

• if you feel that pornography is too difficult to avoid, never feel ashamed to ask for help. God has grace, freedom and support for you—never condemnation. He understands and cares for you and your needs. Looking at porn is a waste of your time. Spending your time with friends, sports, school, church or hobbies is a thousand times more satisfying and good for you.

• if you have ever been uncomfortable from being touched by anyone in the private areas of your body, be sure to tell a trusted adult. Your body is to be respected. A trusted adult can help stop this from happening to you. Don't keep this to yourself.

VI. Wrap Up and Homework

Memorize Gen. 2:24:   "For this reason a man will leave his father and his mother and be united to his wife, and they will become one flesh."

Close with a prayer.

Read Chapter Six: Good Deed Project.

5

Good Deed Project

Christian manhood shows God's love to people through good deeds. Jesus said, "You are the light of the world...Let your light shine before men, that they may see your good deeds and praise your Father in heaven." (Mt. 5:16) James, the brother of Jesus, also teaches that the Christian faith does good works. He said, "Faith by itself, if it is not accompanied by actions, is dead. Show me your faith without deeds, and I will show you my faith by what I do...Faith without deeds is dead." (James 2:17,19-20) The Good Deed Project is an opportunity to show that your faith is alive. People will see your faith with their eyes. They will also see your Father above.

Jesus said "Whoever wants to become great among you must be your servant. For even the Son of Man did not come to be served, but to serve." (Mark 10:42-45) Be the greatest. Serve others. You are not only great when you do good deeds, but you will feel great too. When you bless others, you will also feel blessed. There is joy in giving. Helping others is rewarding.

God will also reward you in this life and the next. Jesus notices when you are kind to others. He taught that "whatever you did for the least of these brothers of mine, you did for me. For I was hungry and you gave me something to eat, I was thirsty and you gave me something to drink, I was a stranger and you invited me in, I needed clothes and you clothed me, I was sick and you looked after me, I was in prison and you came to visit me." (Mt. 25:40,35-36) Consider how you can do these things throughout your lifetime.

Your Good Deed Project can be nearly anything that serves others. Brainstorm with your parents or Mentor Team. Choose a deed that is outside of your home. Taking out the trash, cleaning the dishes or your bedroom is not just a good deed but also a basic responsibility in a family—it's your job. Making your bed every morning is a good habit. Outside of your home, good deeds are limitless. Send a thank you card to someone like a teacher, coach or pastor. Tell them how they have helped you. Feed the hungry. Raise some money from ten friends and send it to a ministry like World Vision. Collect some groceries from friends and take it to a local shelter or food bank. Visit the sick or elderly in a nursing home. For more ideas and inspiration, watch the movie *Pay It Forward* with your family or Mentor Team.

When you touch other people in need, you also touch God's heart. Don't be self-centered. Life is not all about you. Life is about loving and serving. Make giving a way of life. Make this good deed project only the first of a million more good deeds to come.

Good Deed Review

Answer the following questions after you have completed your good deed.

1.   What was your good deed?

2.   How did you feel when you did your good deed?

3.   What did the receiver of your good deed say or do?

4.   What did you learn from your good deed project?

6

Your Role in God's Epic Story: The Four Quarters of the Faith

The early Christians did not originally call themselves "Christians." They called themselves "Followers of the Way." (Acts 9:2, 19:9,23, 22;4,24:14,22) It's still a great name. This lesson about the Christian faith will help you follow the Way and have a better knowledge of your faith. Jesus said, "I am the Way, the Truth, and the Life."(John 14:6). You can't get lost following him.

There are two opposing ways to go in life. As Jesus said, one leads to destruction, while his way leads to life (Mt. 7:13). God offers the better way for his followers. It is a way of love, a way of grace, a way of hope, and a way of peace. Paul even describes Christian love as "the most excellent way." (I Cor. 13:1)

God has also led the way for people throughout human history. His love and grace is seen from the beginning of time to the end of time. Like time in a football game, this history of the world can be divided into four quarters. Today we are living in the fourth quarter, and as in most games, the fourth is usually the most exciting. Jesus is still moving through time, and Christian men have a major role to play in this last and epic quarter of history.

Followers of the Way have a unique goal. They want everyone—including their opponents—to win in life. This is God's goal. Christians don't divide between winners and losers. They even root for and support the opposing teams. They love their enemies. Jesus is not a typical Way. His goal is to take everyone to his eternal side. He is not only the Head Coach of all, he owns the field and everyone on the field. He created everything and everyone. He invites everyone to cross the goal line to the best life in this world and eternal life in the next.

The Four Quarters of the Faith is a brief summary of the Christian faith. While the typical Bible is about 1,900 pages, this summary is only four pages (and very easy to remember). Some churches teach these lessons in confirmation classes for months or years by pastors and teachers. This lesson is also recommended to be taught by a pastor. A test is also included which a pastor can discuss with you. Your pastor will ask you the questions and you will answer them verbally. You will also need to memorize and recite four Scriptures from each Quarter. If there is no pastor involved, your Mentor Team can give you the lesson and test instead. You will study many different subjects in school. This lesson of God's role in world history is worth learning more than any other. Christian manhood starts with knowing Christ and knowing his Word. This lesson helps you know the Bible's epic story. And you are in it.

The Christian Faith in Four Quarters

The First Quarter: Creation

The game begins. God created the world and human beings. After each day of creation God "saw that it was good." Adam is told to take care of the garden of Eden and meets his companion Eve. The First Quarter shows how the world was created to be — all good.

First Quarter Scriptures

"In the beginning God created the heavens and the earth." Gen 1:1

"God created man in his own image, in the image of God he created him, male and female he created them." Gen 1:27

"God saw all that he had made and it was very good." Gen 1:31

"The Lord God took the man and put him in the Garden of Eden to work it and take care of it." Gen. 2:15

The Second Quarter: The Fumble and Fall

God gave Adam and Eve simple instructions. He told them to not eat from the tree of the knowledge of good and evil. They defied his authority and ate from it. They wanted to be like God and decide for themselves what was right and wrong. This was the first or original sin.

Human nature still defies God's commands. Since creation, humans have chosen evil instead of good, choosing wrong instead of right. Like our first parents, we also want to be our own judge of good and evil and do whatever we want. We don't want to be judged—even by God. We are self-centered vs. God-centered. This sinful rebellion since Adam has separated people from God and from each other. Mankind fumbled. The Second Quarter shows how evil and self-centeredness damaged a good world.

Second Quarter Scriptures

"So the Lord God banished him (Adam/man) from the Garden of Eden." Gen 3:23

"Sin entered the world through one man, and death through sin, and in this way death came to all men, because all sinned." Rom. 5:12

"All have sinned and fall short of the glory of God." Ro 3:23

"If we claim to be without sin, we deceive ourselves and the truth is not in us." I John 1:8

The Third Quarter: Redemption

Jesus came to rescue us and bring us back to him. He brings us back into a new garden and back into our original union with our Father. He rescues us from ourselves, death, and condemnation. He took our place on the cross as a sacrifice for our sins. He took our punishment for sins upon himself. We are now free and blameless. Adam's sinful defiance and our own defiance and fumbles are forgiven. God adopts us as his sons and even calls us friends. The Third Quarter shows how God's Son came to find us and rescue us from sin and death.

Third Quarter Scriptures

"For God so loved the world that he gave his one and only Son, that whoever believes in him shall not perish but have eternal life." John 3:16

"This is how God showed his love among us: He sent his one and only Son into the world that we might live through him. This is love, not that we loved God, but that he loved us and sent his Son as an atoning sacrifice for our sins." I John 4:9-10

"For he has rescued us from the dominion of darkness and brought us into the kingdom of the Son he loves, in whom we have redemption, the forgiveness of sins." Col. 1:13

"It is by grace you have been saved, through faith." Eph. 2:8

"Once you were alienated from God and were enemies in your minds as shown by your evil behavior. But now he has reconciled you by Christ's physical body through death to present you holy in his sight, without blemish and free from accusation." Col. 1:21-22

The Fourth Quarter: Restoration of the World

It's time to go on the offense. Now is the time for the triumph of good over evil. You have a mission to restore the world with the good news of God's love, forgiveness, and acceptance. Daily touch other's hearts with your faith and good works. Be a part of God's rescue plan. Show others the Way to the goal and end zone of life. Nothing—not even the gates of hell—can stop God's love and restoration of this world. Jesus will return and make a new heaven and a new earth someday. Your mission is to join the final offensive play of God's love for others. The Fourth Quarter shows our purpose to restore the world to its original goodness and original relationship with our Father.

Fourth Quarter Scriptures

"Go and make disciples of all nations, baptizing them...and teaching them to obey everything I have commanded you. And surely I am with you always, to the very end of the age." (Jesus' last words before ascending into heaven). Mt. 28:19-20.

"If anyone is in Christ, he is a new creation; the old has gone, the new has come. All this is from God, who reconciled us to himself through Christ and gave us the ministry of reconciliation: that God was reconciling the world to himself in Christ, not counting men's sins against them. And he has committed to us the message of reconciliation." (2 Cor 5:17-19)

"See to it that no one misses the grace of God" He 12:15

"Bless those who persecute you; bless and do not curse...Do not be overcome by evil, but overcome evil with good." Rom. 12:14,21

"And I tell you that you are Peter, and on this rock I will build my church, and the gates of Hell will not stand up to it." Matthew 16:18

"Then I saw a new heaven and a new earth, for the first heaven and the first earth had passed away...And I heard a loud voice from the throne say, "Now the dwelling of God is with men, and he will live with them...He will wipe every tear from their eyes. There will be no more death or mourning or crying or pain, for the old order of things has passed away. He who was seated on the throne said, "I am making all things new...I am the Alpha and the Omega, the Beginning and the End. He who overcomes will inherit all this, and I will be his God and he will be my son." Rev. 21:1-7

Ten Questions about the Christian Faith

1. Name the Four Quarters of the Christian Faith.

    First Quarter:

    Second Quarter:

    Third Quarter:

    Fourth Quarter:

2. Which Quarter do we live in today?

3. What did God say about the world he made in the First Quarter?

4. How did Adam and Eve destroy their lives in the Second Quarter?

5. What was the main sin of Adam and Eve — and our own human nature?

6. How do you know God forgave you and loves you in the Third Quarter?

7. What is God's message and mission for you to do in the Fourth Quarter?

8. How do we overcome evil?

9. Good deeds are an example of playing offense in the fourth quarter. What is a good deed that you have done lately?

10. Recite four Scriptures from memory, one from each of the Four Quarters of the Faith. Don't worry if you fumble or forget—your pastor and God will be graceful. Do your best to memorize four. Write four Scriptures here:

One Scripture from the First Quarter:

One Scripture from the Second Quarter:

One Scripture from the Third Quarter:

One Scripture from the Fourth Quarter:

7

Adventure Challenge

A dventure is in men's blood. It's not a surprise that the most popular movies for boys and men are action and adventure movies. What are some of your favorites? Men love challenging adventures and even take risks with their very lives. A scientist with Google named Alan Eustace just had an adventure like this. He floated up to the stratosphere dangling from a balloon in a spacesuit. At 25 miles high, where it is black and the earth below has a curve, he detached himself. He came straight down at 822 miles per hour, breaking the sound barrier and making two sonic booms. Yes, he even survived. If something sounds unbelievable—even insane—men will usually try it.

Your rite of passage also has an adventure to challenge your courage, endurance and abilities (you just won't be sent to space). Adventures stretch you. Your confidence grows when you finish a race, summit a mountain, navigate a river or sail an ocean. You go on to face other challenges in life, such as trying out for a sports team, going to college, finding a job, getting married and raising a family.

Your adventure will be planned together with your Mentor Team. The young men on your team will give their suggestions, but the Mentors will make the final preparations. The Adventure Challenge will be outdoors and preferably include an overnight campout. Tribal rites of passage do the same. They take boys away from their mothers and away from the comforts of home, such as mom's cooking and a comfortable bed. Out in the wilderness, tribes tested a boy to survive by himself and to learn life lessons from older men.

Men throughout the Bible also left the comforts of home behind to find God in the wild. Moses encountered God in the Sinai desert. Isaiah heard God's voice in a cave. Paul's journeys as a missionary included three ship wrecks and floating a day and night in the open sea. When Jesus started his ministry, he was taken out into the desert "with the wild animals" for forty days and nights without any food, while being tempted by Satan. (Mark 1:13)

Open your heart, ears and eyes to God while outside on your adventure. Look up at the stars where "the heavens declare the glory of God." (Psalm 19:1) Listen for God to speak to you through his creation and through the other boys and men.

Be creative as you plan your adventure in the great outdoors. Take a long bike ride, kayak down a river, hike into the woods, summit a mountain, or sail on a lake or ocean. If your day ends with an overnight campout, your Adventure may also include the Initiation into Manhood Ceremony with Fire. What better way to start off your new manhood than after a challenging adventure?

The Christian life calls you to the biggest adventure and challenge in the world. You have a great mission in life. Your faith will face many challenges. You will face battles against yourself, a self-centered culture, and sometimes evil from hell itself. When you battle, always remember the Lord's words that he repeated over and over again to his followers, "Don't be afraid." And before he was arrested, Jesus said, "In this world you will have trouble. But take heart! I have overcome the world." (John 16:33) Paul, who was constantly persecuted for his faith, encourages all of us, "Do not be overcome by evil, but overcome evil with good." (Ro. 12:21

Challenge yourself not only on adventures in mountains or oceans but also to make the world a better place. Spread God's love around wherever you go. Overcome evil with good. If you fail at anything in life, get up, get over it, and try again. Major League baseball players strike out over half the time, but keep going up to bat anyway. Have patience, courage and faith in all you do.

Remember that God is with you wherever you are. As David said, "Where can I go from your Spirit? Where can I flee your presence? If I go up to the heavens, you are there; if I make my bed in the depths, you are there. If I rise on the wings of the dawn, if I settle on the far side of the sea, even there your hand will guide me, your right hand will hold me fast." (Psalm 139:7-10) God is with you even if you go up to space attached to a balloon—but why push it?

Make your whole life a great adventure. Meet new people often. Try new things in school, sports or music. Get out and see new places. Travel whenever possible. Challenge yourself to learn new languages. Don't be a boring couch potato. The world is full of rich experiences. Get out there. Have a great adventure with your team.

Adventure Challenge Review

Answer the following questions after your adventure.

1. What did you and the Mentor Team do for your adventure?

2. What was a challenge on your adventure?

3. What was the most fun on your adventure?

4. What skills or attitudes helped you on your adventure?

5. How can you apply these skills or attitudes to other areas of your life? (like school, sports, music, family)

8

Initiation into Manhood
Fire Ceremony

This will be the shortest chapter of the book because your initiation ceremony is mostly a secret for now. The Mentor Team is planning your ritual. All you probably need to know is that it will not be painful like a tribal initiation. No circumcisions, hot coals, fire ants or scars (you are so lucky!). The ritual will be a special time for the Mentor Team to give you their final instructions and blessings as they initiate you into manhood.

You and the other boys are ready to become men. You have now learned six Lessons of Manhood, the Four Quarters of the Faith, completed a Good Deeds project and have done (or will do) the Adventure Challenge. Now the Mentor Team has one last task—to give you their final instructions, blessings and gifts as they initiate you into manhood.

Remember this moment for the rest of your life. After your initiation, you will never have to guess anymore when you became a man. This ceremony will mark your clear crossing from boyhood to manhood. You will be recognized as a young man. To help you remember the ceremony, complete the following questions when you return.

Mentor Team Initiation Ceremony into Manhood

1. Where was your initiation?

2. Who was there?

3. What were three words of instruction or blessings that you remember from the Mentors?

4.   What gift did you receive? What was the meaning of the gift?

5.   What did you like the most about the ceremony?

6.   How did you feel to be recognized as a man?

9

Church Initiation Ceremony

Your first act of manhood will be to contribute to your Sunday church service—just as the Bar Mitzvah requires young Jewish men to contribute to their Sabbath service. As Paul wrote, "As we have opportunity, let us do good to all people, especially to those who belong to the family of believers." (Gal. 6:10) This will be a good deed to your family of believers.

The date of your Sunday service will be decided by your Pastor and Mentor Team, but will probably be around your birthday (thirteenth or later). The Pastor or one of the Mentors will introduce you to the church and announce that you have completed the training for your Rite of Passage from boyhood to manhood. Your part will take less than five minutes (so no sweat!). You will easily survive the five minutes and the church will be very thankful for your contribution.

You will have three responsibilities; to teach, read and pray. The first part is to teach about one thing—anything--that you learned about Christian manhood in your Crossing Rite of Passage. Also share your chosen Code of Honor. Your speech can be less than two minutes and you can read it from notes if you want to write it down. Your speech will bless and inspire others.

The next duty is to read the Scripture reading of the day. Your pastor will assign you the Scripture, or you may be invited to read a Scripture of your own choice. Your last duty is to lead the church in prayer, either with the Lord's Prayer or by one of your own. If you prefer, you may also write out your prayer and read from your notes.

After your contribution, the pastor may give his or her own recognition and blessing upon your new life as a man. The church may even applaud with their approval and blessing. Either way, you can feel good that you blessed the church with your good deed. The church or family members may even celebrate later with a reception or lunch for you. Blessings on your first act of service as a young man.

Church Service Contribution

Write your notes on this page or your own paper.

Teach: One lesson you learned about Christian manhood.
Also share your chosen Code of Honor.

Read: Read the Scripture of the Day or choose your own.

Pray: Lead the church in the Lord's Prayer or pray your own
prayer for God to bless the church.

Last Blessings for the New Young Men

You did it! Congratulations on completing your rite of passage into manhood. Now continue to contribute to your church and the world for the rest of your life. Your life and gifts are unique and priceless. Don't hide them.

Share your talents with others.

You have a mission to further God's kingdom of grace on earth. People need God's grace. Make sure to give it often.

Serve and protect with the power of a King and the courage of a Warrior.

Honor and respect girls and women.

Enjoy the great adventure of manhood.

Remember that being a man instead of a boy is a choice. Choose manhood every day of your life.

And whenever you strike out, never give up or quit. Go back up to the plate again.

Welcome to the Major Leagues!

Richard Rupp, M.Div., MFT
www.thecrossingnriteofpassage.com

Young Men's Rite of Passage Review

Answer the following questions after you have completed the entire rite of passage. The questions will help you remember all that you learned. The same Review will be collected by your Mentor Team to help them prepare the next team of mentors and boys.

1. As you look back over your whole journey in The Crossing Rite of Passage, what are three things that you liked the most?

    1.

    2.

    3.

2. What are three lessons that you learned about Christian manhood?

    1.

    2.

    3.

3. What is your Code of Honor?

    _____, _____, _____

4. What did you learn from the Adventure Challenge?

5. What did you like most about the Mentor Team Initiation into Manhood Ceremony?

6. What does great manhood do for others?

7. Who are two people who support and care for you--that you can talk to about your needs?

Congratulations on becoming a young man. Go in God's grace, peace, and power. Serve like a good king. Protect like a warrior. Love with honor. Keep the faith. May God bless your life. Have a great adventure!

APPENDIX A

Sixth Century Signing Prayer and Anointing with Oil

Receive the seal of Christ, listen to the divine words, be enlightened by the Word of the Lord, because today you are accepted by Christ.

I sign your forehead in the name of the Father, the Son, and the Holy Spirit so that you may be a Christian.

I sign your eyes so that you may see the glory of God.

I sign your ears so that you may hear the voice of the Lord.

I sign your nostrils so that you may breathe the fragrance of Christ.

I sign your lips so that you may speak the words of life.

I sign your shoulders so that you may bear the yoke of Christ's service.

I sign your whole body, in the name of the Father, the Son and the Holy Spirit so that you may live forever and ever.[11]

Wisdom for Young Men

The Bible is full of wisdom for your life. It gives priceless direction and understanding for a prosperous and successful life. Joshua said, "Do not let this Book of the Law depart from your mouth; meditate on it day and night, so that you may be careful to do everything written in it. Then you will be prosperous and successful." (Jos. 1:8) Write God's commands "on the tablet of your heart" (Pr. 7:3) through memorizing Scripture. One easy way to memorize a verse or chapter is to write down the first letter of each word on a note card for your pocket or a text to yourself on your cell phone. The verse, "Be quick to listen, slow to speak" would be written "Bqtlsts." Give it a try sometime. This trick helps your brain to remember the words. The following verses give priceless wisdom and knowledge on many different topics.

Your Origin and Image

"In the beginning, God created the heavens and the earth." Gen. 1:1

"Then God said, "Let us make man in our image, in our likeness, ...so God created man in his own image, in the image of God he created him, male and female he created them." Gen. 1:26-27

Courage

"Have I not commanded you? Be strong and courageous. Do not be terrified; do not be discouraged, for the Lord your God will be with you wherever you go." Joshua 1:9

Evil

"Those who love the Lord hate evil." Psalm 97:10

"Do not be overcome by evil. Overcome evil with good." Rom. 12:21

Ups and Downs in Life

"There is a time for everything...a time to weep and a time to laugh, a time to mourn and a time to dance." Ecclesiastes 3:4

"Jesus wept." Jn. 11:35

Your Language

"Rid yourselves of all such things as these: anger, rage, malice, slander, and filthy language from your lips." Col. 3:8

"Do everything without complaining or arguing." Php. 2:14

Work

"A man reaps what he sows." Gal. 6:7

"If a man will not work, he shall not eat." 2 Thes. 3:10

Friends

"Two are better than one...If one falls down, his friend can help him up." Eccl 4:9-10

"A friend loves at all times." Prov. 17:17

Choosing Friends

"Bad company corrupts good character." I Cor 15:33

"If sinners entice you, do not give in to them. If they say, "Come along with us; let's lie in wait for someone's blood, let's waylay some harmless soul...my son, do not go along with them, do not set foot on their paths." Prov. 1:10-11,15

Sin

"Confess your sins to each other and pray for each other so that you may be healed." Jas 5:16

"If we confess our sins, he is faithful and just and will forgive us our sins." I John 1:9

The Cross

But they shouted, "Take him away! Take him away! Crucify him!"... So the soldiers took charge of Jesus. Carrying his own cross, he went out to the place of the Skull.. Here they crucified him." John 19:15, 17-18.

"He himself bore our sins in his body on the tree, so that we might die to sins and live for righteousness; by his wounds you have been healed." I Pe. 2:24

"If anyone would come after me, he must deny himself and take up his cross daily and follow me." Luke 9:23

Forgiveness

"Forgive as the Lord forgave you." Col. 3:13

"As far as the east is from the west, so far has he removed our transgressions from us." Ps. 103:12

Grace

"Make sure that no one misses out on God's grace." Heb. 12:15

"Let your conversation be always full of grace." Col. 4:6

Eternal Life

"For God so loved the world that he gave his one and only Son, that whoever believes in him shall not perish but have eternal life." Jn. 3:16

Love

"Love the Lord your God with all your heart and with all your soul and with all your strength." Dt. 6:5

"Love one another. As I have loved you, so you must love one another." John 13:34

Humility

"Do not think of yourself more highly than you ought." Rom 12:3

"Clothe yourselves with compassion, kindness, humility, gentleness and patience." Col. 3:12

Sex and Marriage

"The Lord God said, "It is not good for the man to be alone. I will make a helper suitable for him." Gen. 2:18

"For this reason a man will leave his father and mother and be united with his wife, and they will become one flesh. The man and his wife were both naked, and they felt no shame." Gen. 2:25

Self-Control

"Now Joseph was well-built and handsome, and after a while his master's wife took notice of Joseph and said, 'Come to bed with me!' But he refused." Gen. 39:6-8

"Encourage the young men to be self-controlled." Titus 2:6

Wisdom

"Get wisdom, get understanding...Do not forsake wisdom, and she will protect you; love her, and she will watch over you. Wisdom is supreme; therefore get wisdom. Though it cost all you have, get understanding." Pr. 4:5-7

"Wisdom will save you from the ways of wicked men.. It will save you also from the adulteress." Pr. 2:12,16

Greatness

"Whoever wants to become great among you must be your servant...for even the Son of Man did not come to be served, but to serve." Mk. 10:45

"Whoever practices and teaches these commandments will be called great in the kingdom of heaven." Mt. 5:1

ENDNOTES

[1] Jessica Garrison and Lee Romney, "Boater Drifts 4 Months at Sea," *Los Angeles Times*, B1, September 25, 2002.

[2] Jeffrey Salkin, Putting God on the Guest List: How to Reclaim the Spiritual Meaning of Your Child's Bar or Bat Mitzvah (Woodstock: Jewish Lights Publishing, 1996) 7.

[3] Salkin 63.

[4] Salkin 63.

[5] David Gilmore, *Manhood in the Making: Cultural Concepts of Masculinity* (New Haven: Yale University: 1990) 13.

[6] Gordon Dalbey, *Healing the Masculine Soul* (Nashville: W Publishing Group, 2003) 29.

[7] Robert Bly, *Iron John.* (New York: Addison-Wesley Publishing Company, 1990) 32.

[8] Dr. Steve Perry Explains Why Many Fatherless Sons Join Gangs https://www.huffingtonpost.com/2013/07/22/steve-perry-fatherless-sons-gangs_n_3623690.html (video)

[9] Bly 15.

[10] Arthur McCormack, *Christian Initiation* (New York: Hawthorn Books, 1969) 95.

[11] McCormack 50.

ABOUT THE AUTHOR

Richard Rupp, M.Div., MFT started following the Way by age thirteen. Rick is a licensed Marriage & Family Therapist with a private practice in Pasadena, CA. A graduate of Fuller Theological Seminary, he has also taught as an adjunct professor on Psychotherapy with Men. Rick speaks to men's retreats and marriage conferences on men's issues, sex and romance, and grace-filled marriages. His counseling practice helps men and women find the most excellent way to love.

Rick is also CEO of WayPoint Sailing, a corporate teambuilding sailboat racing company with sails on the Pacific Ocean. For Mentor Teams in Southern California, he also arranges sails to Catalina Island for The Crossing Rite of Passage. Set sail at www.waypointsailing.com.

Rick lives in Los Angeles with his beloved wife and is the proud father of a daughter and son. His son was among the first team of boys to successfully complete the Crossing into Manhood.

Rick can be contacted at:
www.thecrossingriteofpassage.com

Made in the USA
Middletown, DE
11 August 2019